HANAUMA DAY

A Legend of Arm Wrestling

LONG AGO, TWO HAWAIIAN WARRIORS WERE IN LOVE WITH THE SAME BEAUTIFUL GIRL.

A GIRL WHOSE BEAUTY WAS KNOWN THROUGHOUT THE ISLANDS.

THE GIRL'S FATHER WAS A KAHUNA, A PRIEST WHO DREW HIS POWER FROM A MAGIC LIZARD OR MO'O.

4

THE BEAUTIFUL GIRL WORRIED THAT THE TWO WARRIORS WOULD DIE SO SHE TURNED HERSELF INTO A TALL VOLCANIC MOUNTAIN, IN ORDER THAT BOTH MEN WOULD BE ABLE TO LOOK UPON HER BEAUTY FOREVER.

WHEN HER FATHER LEARNED WHAT SHE HAD DONE HE WEPT AND PRAYED TO HIS GODS.

GREAT MO'O HELP ME!

THEN HE CURLED HIMSELF UP AT THE BASE OF THE CRATER TO PROTECT THE SPIRIT OF HIS DAUGHTER FOREVER. THE GODS CHANGED HIM INTO THE SHAPE OF A MO'O.

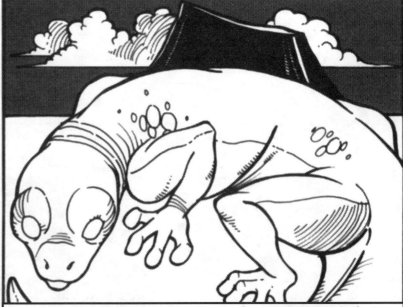

THIS IS WHY THE HANAUMA BAY LOOKS THE WAY IT DOES, AND WHY IT WAS NAMED HANAUMA, "ARM WRESTLING BAY".

A scientific version of the same story.

The Island of Oʻahu was formed 2-3 million years ago. But Hanauma Bay did not exist until much later. In its place was a coral reef, probably fronting a beautiful white sand beach. Approximately 30,000 years ago, lava under tremendous pressure forced itself up through the earth's crust, making a crack three miles long across the reef. When the hot lava mixed with the cold sea water, great explosions occurred, sending plumes of hot steam, ash, and coral miles into the sky.

As the ash and bits of coral fell and cooled, they hardened into three tuft cone craters at the edge of the sea. The ash sealed off two craters from the ocean, Koko Head and Koko Crater, but large waves striking the seaward rim of the middle crater, kept it open to the ocean and created Hanauma Bay. Walking down the road to the Bay, you can see small white bits of coral embedded in the face of the cliff and rock ledges. These are remnants of the original coral reef embedded in volcanic ash rock.

How did they know?

Both the ancient Hawaiian and the modern scientific stories have one significant fact in common. Both describe the creation of Hanauma Bay and Koko Head long after the main island of Oʻahu had formed. The scientist's version is based on years of research, rock samples and scientific methods. The ancient Hawaiians had none of these tools yet reached a similar conclusion. Their methods remain a mystery.

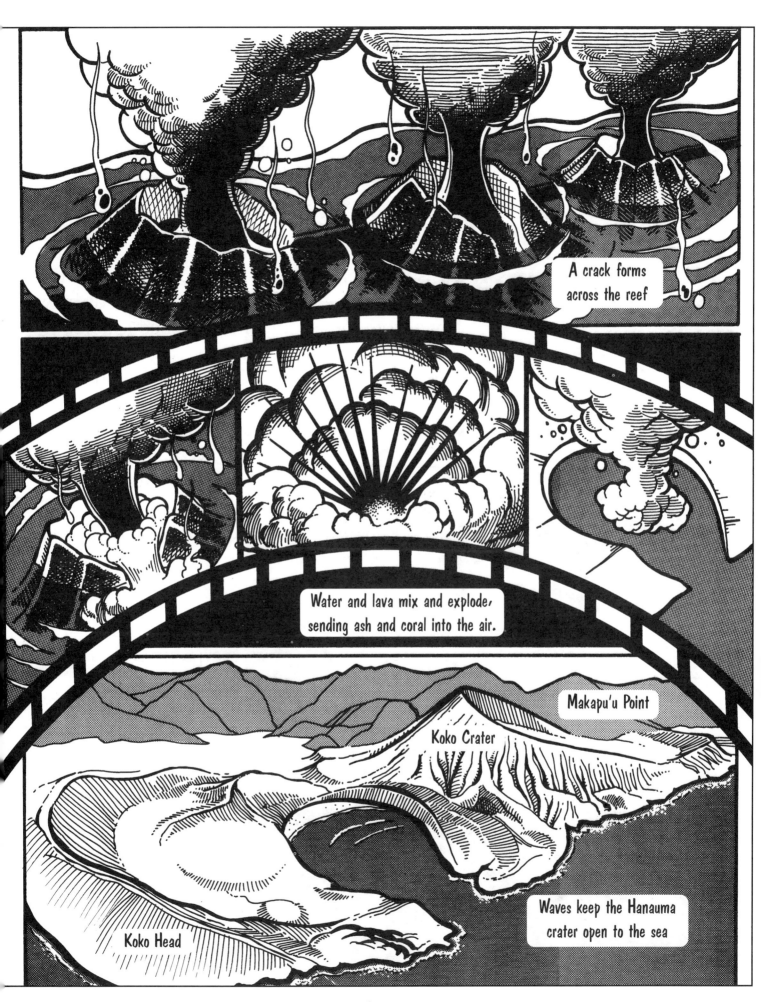

How The Plants Arrived

The new tuft cone surface was hot and lifeless. But within days insects began to crawl across the cooling surface. The first plants to settle came from the adjoining landmass and were probably blue green algae. The algae were followed by lichens, ferns, and mosses. Approximately half of all native plants in Hawaii arrived with birds as seeds deposited in bird droppings or in dirt attached to feet or feathers. Other seeds blew down from the jet stream or washed ashore.

After thousands of years, clusters of coastal plants specially adapted to dry areas, such as coastal sandalwood, took root and prospered in the Hanauma Bay area. But few of the native plants were edible to humans. In order to survive in this new environment, the early Polynesian settlers brought plants in their canoes, like taro, coconut trees, and sweet potato, that would provide food.

Of the 957 varieties of native Hawaiian flowering plants, 851 are not naturally found anywhere else on earth.

People Come to the Bay

The first Polynesians sailed canoes to Hawaii in about the year 300 AD. The early settlers are believed to have come from the Marquesas Islands 3,500 miles to the south. At that point in time few other people in the world had the skill or knowledge to sail such great distances across the open ocean.

Most of the settlements in Hawaii were in areas with abundant fresh water (such as near the springs in Hawaii Kai). But protected bays like Hanauma were important fishing centers, even though they had no fresh water.

A 1952 archaeological dig at Hanauma Bay revealed the remains of a communal fishing shelter used for several hundred years. Scientists found the remains of ancient campfires, fish hooks and tools. The ancient Hawaiians used the spines of pencil urchins to file fish hooks from pig, dog, bird, and human bones. The hooks were made in a number of styles, each sharpened to catch a certain kind of fish. According to legend the best hooks were made from the bones of brave or hairless men skilled in martial arts. This is one of the reasons why the ancient Hawaiians went to great lengths to hide the bones of departed loved ones. Family members did not want their relatives to end up as someone's prized fish hook.

Land And Sea

The ancient Hawaiians believed, that certain land plants had a twin seaweed with a similar sounding name living in the ocean. This belief had a practical use. The ancient Hawaiians had great skill in the use of native plants and seaweeds to treat medical problems. It was common practice for native Hawaiian healers to give a patient in the final stage of treatment (*pani* in Hawaiian), the seaweed that was the matching twin of the land plant instrumental in making the treatment effective. The pairing of land and sea, an important part of the *Kumulipo*, the Hawaiian creation myth, completed the treatment.

Why the plants were important

The Hawaiians needed plants for survival. Some fishermen were skilled at catching fish using a narcotic plant called *auhuhu* (<u>Tephrosia</u> <u>purpurea</u>). They would gather the plant, crush it, and then put it in tide pools. Fish in the pools would be drugged by the toxin and float stunned to the surface. But the effect lasted only about twenty minutes. Any fish that weren't gathered for food, would recover and swim away unharmed.

There is no indication that the toxin in the fish ever affected the humans who ate them.

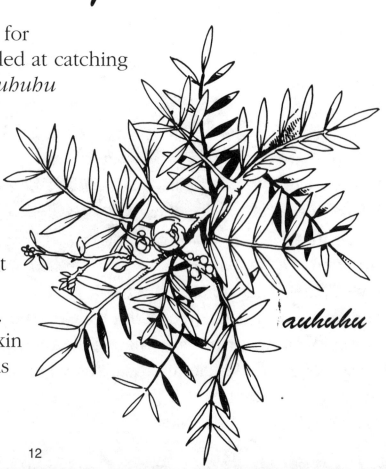

auhuhu

12

Fish travel long distances to Hawaii

The ancestors of the fish that live in Hanauma Bay originally came from the Philippine Sea, Micronesia, and the tropical seas of Asia. The fish drifted thousands of miles as small eggs and larvae amidst the great masses of plankton borne by currents in the open sea. When the larvae reached Hawaii they settled out of the plankton, dropped onto the reefs and began to grow. The number of fish and type of fish that arrived this way was largely dependent on chance. But once several fish of the same species became established on a reef, their offspring rapidly spread throughout the island chain.

Larvae

day 1

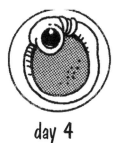

day 2

day 4   1 week   3 weeks

Prepared Fish Hawaiian style.

Ancient Hawaiians enjoyed the natural juices of fish flesh. Believing that cooking (or sometimes killing) a fish would spoil its flavor, they sometimes ate small reef fish alive! Fish were like fine wine each with its own particular flavor depending upon its age, diet, and where it lived.

Fish etiquette

It is considered poor manners in Hawaii to eat *fish* tail first. The *manini*, or convict tang, is a small white surgeonfish with vertical black bars on its sides. Hawaiians are

manini

very particular in the way they eat their fish and to eat a *manini* tail first is, as one fishermen said, "to put one's nose in the air and show disrespect". The correct method was head first.

To supplement the water they carried in gourds while fishing, the Hawaiians sometimes ate fish like the *manini* alive, in order to quench their thirst. The body fluids inside a live fish contain only about one third the salt content of seawater.

Never tell anybody you're going fishing,

Hawaiians believed it was bad luck. Fish might be able to hear you. It also was not a good idea to walk on a sandy beach near where people were fishing, to hold your hands behind you, to eat bananas, or to have a woman step across your net. Fishing was a serious business to the ancient Hawaiians and they were very particular.

Women in Hawaii were seaweed experts.

Prior to 1819, the year Liholiho, King Kamehameha II abolished the *kapu* system, turtles, certain species of fish such as *ulua* and *kumu*, coconuts, and all but three varieties of bananas, were *kapu* to women. These foods were eaten by men only.

In order to supplement their diet women became expert at the gathering of foods such as seaweeds and shellfish on which there were no restrictions. There are 440 different species of seaweed in Hawaii of which all but 50 are edible. Each type of *limu* has its own particular taste. Some are bland, some are peppery, and some are simply pleasant to chew. *Limu* is usually eaten raw as a condiment, although one species (*limu aki'aki*) is baked or used as a thickening agent in stews with chicken or fish.

In the traditional practice of *Ho'oponopono* which is used to settle serious grievances among families, a common brown seaweed, *limu kala* ("to forgive") is used. The seaweed is draped, like an open lei, around the neck of the family member thought by a *kupuna (an* elder) to be responsible for the argument. This individual then enters the ocean, and waits for the crest of a rising wave. The *limu* (symbolizing the cause of the trouble) floats away and leaves the family free to be happy together again.

Limu Kala

Look out point.

A famous hill on the right side of Hanauma Bay called *Mo'okua -O-Kaneapua* was used by Hawaiians as a look-out point. From atop the hill it was possible to see all the way to Molokai and observe any canoes coming towards O'ahu. This was important because the kings of the different Hawaiian Islands were often at war. The hill was also used by travellers before sailing to Molokai across the Kàiwi Channel. Travellers would stop at Hanauma Bay and climb the hill in order to look at wave conditions and the wind direction before they left.

The Magic Stone

One legend of the formation of Hanauma Bay concerns a battle between Madame *Pele*, the volcano Goddess and her older sister, *Namaka O Ka Hai*. Although *Namaka* lost the struggle and fled to the island of Maui, her spirit was said to have remained within a stone on a nearby hillside. According to legend it glows at night when offerings of *awa* (a narcotic drink made from the root of the *awa* plant) are left beside it.

The Moon of Kūkolu

The fifth night of the new moon - called *Kūkolu* —was considered by Hawaiians to be the best time during summer for men to go fishing and was an excellent time for women to dive for sea urchins.

Olonā

Contrary to popular opinion, the ancient Hawaiians did not have thrownets. Thrownets were introduced by Japanese immigrants in the 19th century. The ancient Hawaiians used surround nets made from the lightweight fibers of *olonā* plants to catch fish.   Tests of this endemic Hawaii plant by the US government have shown that it has some of the strongest natural fibers in existence. It was not uncommon for Hawaiian fishing nets made from olonā to last fifty years or more.

Hawaiian Underwater Spears

Fishing spears were made with a hard wood shaft and a point of sharpened bone. They were three to six feet long while those used for octopus were as long as 13 feet ! Some spear fishermen used underwater fish calls - clicking the inside of their cheeks with their tongue to attract fish towards them underwater. The clicking sound emulates the 'pop-pop-pop" sound of small shrimp snapping their claws underwater. Spear fishermen could stay underwater 4-5 minutes at a time and did not wear face masks.

Modern history

After the attack on Pearl Harbor in 1941, Hanauma Bay was considered a possible landing site for Japanese invasion. Defenses were built to repel an invasion and Hanauma Bay was code named Minnesota Beach. James Jones, who would later become famous for writing the novel "From Here to Eternity", was assigned duty here. Because the invasion never came, he and his fellow soldiers grew bored and some threw hand grenades onto the reef to create deeper areas for swimming.

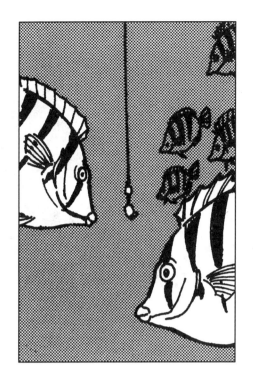

In days past

Hanauma Bay was said to have been a favorite fishing, swimming and picnic area for Hawaiian royalty. King Kamehameha V often fished there. Later a cattle ranch was developed in the surrounding hills and people came from Honolulu to fish and camp. By the mid 1960's, heavy fishing pressure on the reef resulted in depleted fish stocks.

Hanauma Bay became a marine preserve in 1967.

Before 1967 fishing was permitted in Hanauma Bay with all types of equipment; traps, thrownets, poles, spears, and gill nets. The water was clear but the only fish to be seen were too small to be worth catching. The Bay might never have become a marine preserve if it were not for the work of Chapman Lam. During the early 1960's University of Hawaii marine biologist Ernie Reese suggested that Hanauma Bay should be set aside as a kind of living museum. But the idea was not popular. Many fishermen were against converting the Bay into a marine preserve because they feared that it might eventually lead to the closing of other traditional fishing grounds.

Chapman Lam

Lam had returned to Hawaii after 13 years away in the US Navy and noticed that fishing had depleted much of Hawaii's reef life. He decided that Hanauma Bay should be preserved so there would be at least one place in Hawaii where his children and grandchildren might enjoy the ocean as he had. Lam organized an underwater survey of the Bay and used the information to pressure the state government into accepting the plan. In 1967, his efforts were rewarded and the Bay was designated a Marine Life Conservation District.

ABOVE THE BAY

Hunting for fish? Follow the birds!

Seabirds and tuna often appear together, feeding on schools of small baitfish near the surface. For hundreds of years Hawaiian fishermen have looked for hovering flocks of birds as indicators of tuna schools in the ocean. From a small boat, the horizon is only eight miles away. But skilled fishermen can spot the birds in the sky above a school of fish from up to 12 miles away... beyond the horizon!

There are 12 different species of seabirds that follow tuna schools in Hawaiian waters. The seabirds have special oil glands that waterproof their feathers, enabling them to dive for small fish without getting their feathers soaking wet. A few species, such as tropic birds and boobies, are specially adapted to plunge head first into the water at speeds up to 40 mph, in pursuit of fish. Their heads are protected from the shock of the impact by thick bones and special air cushions around their necks.

No native mosquitoes in Hawaii:

Mosquitoes were first recorded in Lahaina, Maui in 1826. They apparently arrived in barrels of drinking water aboard whaling ships. There are now two common mosquito species found at Hanauma Bay; one bites during the day and the other at night. Only female mosquitoes bite. Bird diseases transmitted by mosquitoes are considered one factor in the decline of native Hawaiian birds.

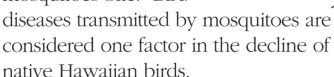

Okay to go fishing? Look at the trees

Fishing from a small canoe could be dangerous in windy weather. But inland, the wind is often blocked by trees and hills. To tell if it's too windy at the beach, Hawaiians would often look to the tallest trees. If the leaves were frolicking, the ocean would sure to be rough.

No Seagulls Here.

There aren't any. Seagulls are found living only on the major continents. Most of the white birds seen at Hanauma Bay are pigeons introduced in the 19th century. However, common Pacific seabirds such as sooty terns, shearwaters and tropic birds can also be seen. Seagulls need greater masses of fish to eat than can be found in Hawaii's waters.

EDGE OF THE SEA

Watch where you walk, especially along the sides of the Bay.

Although the ledges of the Bay look safe, walk on them cautiously because large waves can wash up suddenly and knock the unwary against the cliffs. A number of people have been knocked unconscious and dragged into the water along these ledges by the force of waves. Having your picture taken with waves crashing behind you can be particularly dangerous. Don't turn your back on the ocean is a traditional Hawaiian warning.

The cone shaped shells on the rocks are called 'opihi

Hawaiian limpet ('opihi) like other seafood in Hawaii, are considered best when eaten raw and alive. Unfortunately the demand for these small shellfish has outstripped available supply. The result has been high prices and overharvesting. At Hanauma Bay these shell fish are protected but in most other areas throughout the state 'opihi is found only in remote areas where surf beats against rock. 'Opihi pickers risk their lives, rushing into the rocky areas when the waves are low, prying the 'opihi off the rock with butterknives and then running out before the next set of waves hits. Each year people are killed and injured gathering 'opihi and the price of the delicacy continues to rise.

They caught crabs by tickling them.

Along the shores of Hanauma Bay scores of small black crabs scamper up and down the rocks. The Hawaiians call them 'a'ama crabs (ah-ah-ma). In ancient days they were gathered by the Hawaiians when the seas were too rough to go out fishing. The 'a'ama crabs have eyes that bulge at the end of long flexible eye stalks. This enables them to look in every direction and makes it hard for even the swiftest fishermen to get close to them.

To catch the 'a'ama, ancient Hawaiian fishermen would cut long thin fibers from the spine of a palm frond and create a long thin flexible stick. They would tie a loop at one end of the stick and then use it to reach over the slippery rocks and gently tickle the eye stalk of a crab. The startled crab would respond to the irritation by dropping its long black eye stalk tightly against its side, pinching the thread between the eye and the shell. The Hawaiians would then flick them into a bucket. They were careful to take no more than they needed.

Look out for the salt bowls

Along the rock cliffs you may see small depressions eroded in the rock. These depressions and others made by the Hawaiians were used to collect salt from evaporated sea water. The Hawaiians needed salt to dry their fish so they would have their favorite food during the winter months when the seas were too rough to fish. Dried fish and *poi* with *limu* for flavoring, were for many generations, the principal diet of Hawaiians.

Rock skippers on the ledges

When the tide is low, small goby fish, (ʻoʻopu), may be seen in pools on the rock ledges around the bay. These fish often jump as far as five feet from one tide pool to the next. How do they know which way to jump? When the tide is high, they swim about and memorize the location of each of the pools within a set territory. In this way at low tide gobies can move from pool to pool escaping predators and finding more food. But the gobies won't just jump anywhere. If a goby is picked up and put into an unfamiliar pool, it will not jump out! Hawaiian fishermen would sometimes catch these fish and use them for bait or chew them alive as a tasty snack.

ʻoʻopu

Pencil urchins...

...do not have lead points. They are large red sea urchins (ʻinaʻula) with armor plating. Their spines are tough enough to ward off most of the animals that can attack. Trigger fish pick off the spines one by one and when the urchin is defenseless the trigger fish breaks it open and eats the insides. The spines of pencil urchins were used by fishermen as files to shape fish hooks from bone. The red color from the spines was used to dye tapa cloth.

Medicine in their spines

Along the shore where the surf is strong you may see flattened purple sea urchins with broad dull spines, laid out against the rock. These urchins, *hāʻukeʻuke,* are specially adapted to live in an environment where waves pound against the jagged rocks. The ancient Hawaiians harvested these urchins and ground up their spines for medicine.

Calling someone a sea urchin in ancient Hawaii was considered an insult. It implied a big head with little inside.

hāʻukeʻuke

Sharp spines for protection

Along the nearshore, thousands of tiny white or black short spined sea urchins, *wana,* can be seen in holes burrowed into the reef. The urchins burrow into the reef for protection from predators and crashing waves. In deeper waters outside the reef you may see long-spined black sea urchins. The spines from these urchin are <u>VERY</u> sharp and should not be touched. The shorter spines are hollow and attached to poison glands.

wana

25

Coloring page

Damsel Fish: Farmers of the Reef

During spring and summer, small round splashes of purple can often be seen on some of the underwater rocks. If you look carefully, you will see silver and gray striped fish swimming nearby. These are damsel fish or *mamo* guarding the purple eggs they have glued to the rock face. Other fish such as the *hinalea* will try to dart in and eat the eggs, but the moment they try, the damsel fish will scare them off.

Mamo have an interesting spring courtship ritual. Early in the morning the male *mamo* can be seen changing its color pattern and perform a vigorous acrobatic dance to attract a female. Once a female is attracted, the male leads her to a prepared nest site. The male clears algae from a flat rocky surface, by using its teeth to scrape it clean. The female lays her eggs in the clearing, and they are fertilized by the male. This may be repeated up to a dozen times at one nest site with several females.

Another kind of damsel fish (there are more than 12 in Hawaii) is called a farmer fish. These fish will carefully cultivate a patch of rock to grow certain types of algae that they prefer to eat. They will pluck out weeds (algae they don't want to grow in the patch) and chase away any intruders that might try to move in on their pasture.

Mamo

Feeding Frenzy

Strict fishing regulations combined with the desire of visitors to feed fish have created a feeding frenzy among the Bay's inhabitants. Because there are more fish in Hanauma Bay than on a normal reef, competition for food is fierce. The most aggressive species grow to the largest size. As a result, species such as *'ama'ama* (mullet), *enenue* (rudderfish) and *kala* (surgeon fish) predominate, while other smaller reef inhabitants like *'o'opu* (gobies) are hardly seen. The ever-hungry fish have eaten much of the seaweed that would normally be found on the reef.

The undersea telephone line.

The large cable that runs out through the gap near the center of the reef is a telephone line laid in 1956. Although largely superseded by satellite communications, these kinds of cables are still used by the military because they are harder to tap than satellite transmissions and are much better for security.

Cowrie Shells

Cowrie shells, *leho*, are shiny because their smooth surface is usually covered by a living membrane that lubricates and polishes the shell. Leho shells were used for ornamentation and for octopus lures.

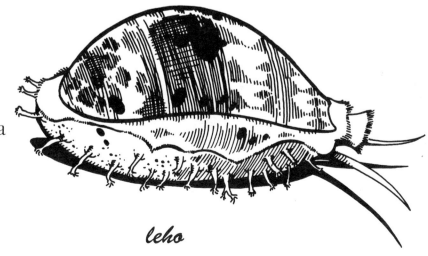

leho

The beginning of a coral reef

When Hanauma Bay was formed, the ocean covered the floor of the crater. Microscopically small coral animals drifted into the Bay from the open sea and cemented themselves onto the rocky floor. Individual coral animals (called polyps) have interconnected digestive tracts, so food that was taken in by one polyp was shared by many. As the coral colony grew upward, sand and debris became trapped and cemented to the colony base eventually forming a reef and raising its level to the surface of the ocean. At Hanauma Bay this process has been going on for more than 20,000 years.

How fast do corals grow?

Less than a quarter inch per year.

Coral Babies

Once a coral colony is established, it reproduces by budding, increasing the size of the coral head one cell at a time. But once a year around midnight on the first full moon of spring all of the coral heads on the reef spew eggs and sperm into the water. Fertilized coral eggs float in the ocean currents until they find a place to settle.

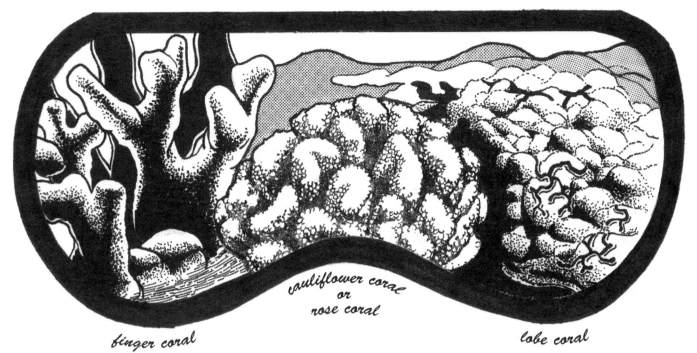

cauliflower coral
or
rose coral

finger coral

lobe coral

Three most common coral

A coral's shape adapts it to certain places on a reef. Finger corals grow upward towards the sun, but grow most successfully in calm deep water. Their thin branches can't withstand the surge of waves nearshore. The greenish lobe coral can form either massive boulders to resist wave surge or thin encrusting colonies to endure turbulent surf. Rose coral forms small branched heads that hold tightly to the rocks and are found in areas of heavy surf and strong currents.

What do corals eat?

Corals eat microscopic sized animals called plankton swimming in ocean waters, but most of their energy comes from the sun! Inside each tiny coral polyp are hundreds of even smaller algae plant cells which produce energy by photosynthesis just like land plants. The algae give the coral head its color. Separate colonies of the same species of coral may be different colors because they are inhabited by different algae.

Coral are different colors

Colors in coral are caused by small plant cells that live and reproduce within the coral tissue. The color of the coral, red, purple, blue, or green, depends upon which photosynthetic pigment the plant cell happens to be born with. Because each coral head starts from a single cell, the mature coral head will be of the same color as the first coral cell.

Coral Cuts

All live corals are coated with a slimy mucus. The mucus pushes away dirt and floating bacteria from the brittle coral surface and makes sure it stays clean. If you get cut by coral, the dirt and bacteria in this mucus will enter the wound. To avoid infection it's a good idea to clean a coral cut with disinfectant. Vinegar is popularly used for this purpose in Hawaii as it will also dissolve any bits of coral skeleton in the wound. Contrary to popular belief, coral does not continue to grow inside the cut.

Sick Coral

The small dirt particles and sediment that falls on coral, blocks the light, oxygen, and food that coral needs to live. To keep itself clean, coral produces a mucus which carries the dirt and sediment to the edge of the colony where it is swept by the ocean current back into the water. But if the amount of sediment that settles everyday is overwhelming, the coral can die from the exhaustion of constantly trying to clean itself.

Dead coral . . .

Much of the shallow flat coral shelf inside the reef is dead. This inner reef has been smoothed and denuded of almost all live coral by humans walking on it. Live coral can be seen at the edges of the reef where humans seldom walk. The slippery film of green slime growing on the inner reef is algae that takes advantage of the nutrients flowing into the bay.

Fish Eyes

The eyes of most reef fish are located on the sides (rather than the front) of their heads. This enables fish to see all the way around, looking for predators. Skilled snorkelers will often pretend to look away from fish they want to get close to. A fish's vision is so acute that even the slightest look, taken as a threat, will send it scurrying to safety.

Many fish have large false eye spots near their tails

The tail spot is intended to look like an eye. Because most large predators instinctively attack by going for the head of their prey, a dot on the tail is a good decoy. The moment a large fish strikes for what it thinks is the eye of its prey, the smaller fish wiggles its tail and swims for safety.

How many fish?

There are about 400 species of fish in Hawaii. A rough estimate puts the number of fish in the Bay at 50,000.

Longest Fish Name.

Humuhumunukunukuāpua'a? No..., but it's close.
The longest fish name is *lauwiliwilinukunuku'oi'oi* — roughly translated, it means "fish like the leaf of the *wili wili* tree with a sharp beak". It is commonly known as the Long Nose Butterfly Fish.

Vacuum cleaner snouts.

With its long nose (actually an elongated mouth) the *lauwiliwilinukunuku'oi'oi* can reach tiny marine organisms like baby crabs and fish larvae that live in the narrow crevices of the reef. When the tip of the mouth is close to its prey, the jaw muscles flex and the small animal gets sucked into a vacuum cleaner like mouth.

Some fish are colorful, Some are not.

Reef fish can see colors and it is likely that the many color patterns on the different species allow fish to tell friend from foe. The color patterns can camouflage fish from their predators, or attract mates during courtship.

The small square looking fish in the Bay

...are called box fish. There are several species of box fish in the Bay. They have tiny fins, lots of spots and are poisonous for people and fish to eat.

Eels have hard heads.

Moray eels (*puhi*) have hard skulls and long leathery bodies covered with slime. Their tough skins allow them to hunt for food among the narrow cracks and holes in the abrasive coral reef. Moray eels have long needle-like teeth designed to penetrate the scales of fish.

In the caves and small reef crevices where the eels live, spiny lobsters (*ula*) are often found. If an *ula* is sharing the same cave as an eel the *ula* will extend one long tentacle forward and one back to warn of the eels approach. If there are no eels in the cave the *ula* will extend both of its long tentacles forward in order to ward off danger from outside the cave.

ula

Moray eels will bite.

Moray eels are not normally aggressive. Most cases of moray eel bites occur when a diver reaches blindly into a coral hole and puts his hand directly into the eel's face. In 1991 State officials removed 70 large eels from Hanauma Bay in order to protect swimmers.

The Mū Story

Mū (a Porgy) is the Hawaiian fish with human-like teeth. Found in moderately deep water, the *mū* eats sea urchins by pulling off one spine at a time until the urchin is stripped of defenses. The *mū* is bluish gray in color with red lips. The ancient Hawaiians considered the fish so frightening that *mū* was the name they gave to their executioners, and according to some sources sacrificial victims were fed *mū* before they were killed. *Mū* is one of the hardest fish to approach because of its sharp vision and quick reflexes. However, *mū* can be attracted by making clicking noises to simulate the sound of small shrimp.

mū

Octopus - more intelligent than dogs?

If you look closely at the ocean bottom, you may see a pair of eyes watching you from atop a coral rock. But approach too closely and the rock will change color, sprout eight arms and slither off to a hole in the reef. Octopus, (*he'e*), are masters of camouflage and are among the most intelligent animals on the reef. Marine scientists say octopus are about as intelligent as dogs. They have been trained to enter and leave spaces as tight as coke bottles - after removing the cork, of course! Local fishermen refer to octopus as squid. A fisherman adept at locating octopus on the reef is said to possess a keen "squid eye."

The Octopus is the master of camouflage

he'e

The big gray fish near the beach.

Enenue or Rudder Fish are common in the nearshore waters of the Bay because they are aggressive and have adapted well to the feed offered by visitors. Normally *enenue* are found on the outer edge of the reef in deeper water. They are known for having an unusually strong odor.

enenue

Why some fish are silver

Silver fish, like the Hawaiian Flagtail (*aholehole)* reflect light off their shiny scales. To a seabird flying above, a large school of silver fish blends with the sunlight reflecting off the waters surface. In the water, the silver scales reflect background color. The reflections break up the fishes' silhouettes underwater and make them difficult to see by a potential predator.

Fish ears

Fish have tiny bones in their heads called otoliths that vibrate like tuning forks in response to sound. Because an otolith grows larger by adding one layer per day, scientists can judge the age of a fish by counting the rings in the otolith bone - the same way you can age a tree by counting its rings.

Goat fish have whiskers?

Goat fish or *weke* are named for the whisker-like barbells extending from their lower jaw. These tentacles are very sensitive to smell and touch. Goat fish use them to detect tiny crabs and other animals living beneath the sand or hidden in coral reefs.

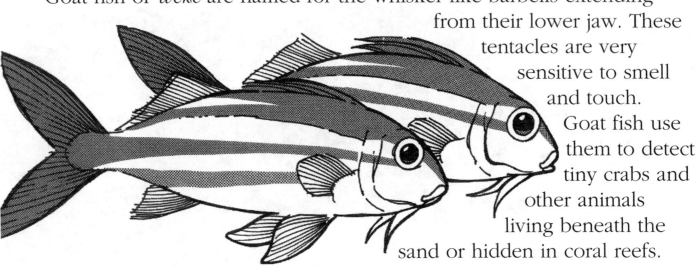

Nightmare weke

The common white goat fish with black chevrons on its tail is called *weke pahulu* in Hawaiian, "nightmare *weke*". This fish contains a chemical that can cause hallucinations when eaten. There have been a number of articles written in Hawaii medical journals regarding patients who have suffered bad dreams as a result of eating this fish. The head and intestines have the highest levels of toxins. Despite this side effect, this fish is commonly sold in local fish markets.

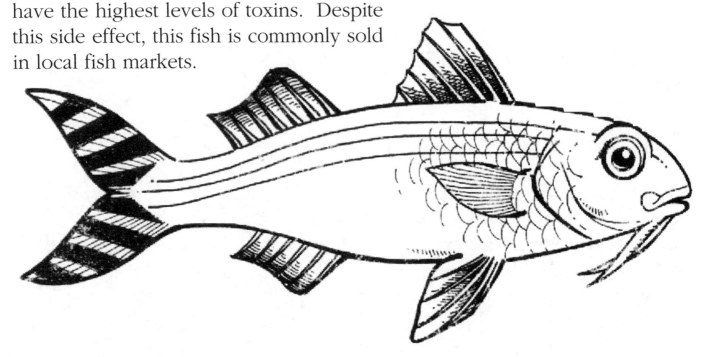

Parrot fish don't talk...

...but their crunching can be heard across the Bay. Parrot fish use their beak-like teeth to scrape off small chunks of coral and algae. Hard, flat grinder bones inside their throats pulverize the coral to help digest the tiny animals and plants that live inside. What the parrot fish cannot digest is defecated above the reef, leaving long plumes of fine sand in the water as they swim. The ancient Hawaiians were aware of this behavior and called one of the species of parrot fish *uhu pālukaluka* which means uhu with the loose bowels! It is estimated that much of the sand in the Bay (and in Hawaii) is due to *uhu* defecation over thousands of years. The small paired scrape marks on coral heads in the Bay mark where parrot fish have been feeding.

Sexual discrimination.

Male parrot fish are bright green and blue. The females are dull red or brown. Each male will have a harem of several females. When a male parrot fish dies, the dominant female in the harem undergoes a sex change to become the new male. It usually takes three weeks for a drab colored female to turn into a bright blue-green male.

Tattle-Tale parrotfish

Hawaiian fishermen would watch this fish very carefully when out on the reef. If they saw parrot fish in separate groups, they would continue fishing. But if they saw them frolicking in a small group, the fishermen would rush home. It was a sign their wives were being unfaithful.

Wrasse are the most common fish in the Bay,

Hinalea is the common name for several types of wrasses in Hawaii. *Hinalea* have tiny scales and lots of slime. They were offered to the gods in ancient Hawaii to encourage pregnancy and in some cases were fed to mothers in the hope their unborn children would be well behaved. But according to the ancient healers, a *hinalea* treatment always had a side affect. It was said to cause bad breath.

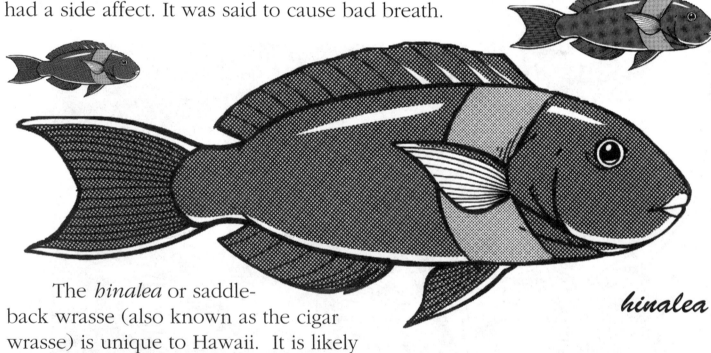

hinalea

The *hinalea* or saddle-back wrasse (also known as the cigar wrasse) is unique to Hawaii. It is likely descended from a few fish that drifted to Hawaii from Indonesia or the Philippines. Over thousands of years it evolved features different from its South Pacific ancestors that enabled it to prosper in Hawaiian waters. Today, it has changed so much from its original ancestors that it is designated an endemic species and lives nowhere else in the world.

Puffer fish toxin is so powerful it can create zombies.

Puffer (*'O'opu-hue*) fish are often seen in the Bay. When they are threatened, they fill their bag-like bodies with sea water and extend their sharp spines. Puffer fish toxin, properly prepared and administered so slows down the rate of human metabolism that people can live for weeks or even months on little food, water or air. In 1986, a Harvard scientist in Haiti discovered that individuals who had ingested pufferfish toxins had such slowed rates of metabolism that they were declared legally dead and actually buried underground! Later they were dug up, given an antidote, and put to work as slaves. People under the influence of the puffer fish toxin in Haiti are called zombies!

'O'opu-hue

Poison or Delicacy?

Called Fugu in Japan, the puffer fish is considered to be a unique combination of food delicacy and dangerous recreational drug. Fugu is said to cause a tingling feeling in the mouth when chewed and a feeling of almost total relaxation when eaten. Unfortunately, the relaxation can be fatal if the fish is not prepared properly. The innards of the fish contain most of the toxin and the fish must be cleaned with care. The poison has a paralyzing effect that is capable of slowing down the rate of breathing until a person dies. In Japan, where Fugu is a delicacy, an average of 150 people die every year from Fugu poisoning. There is no antidote.

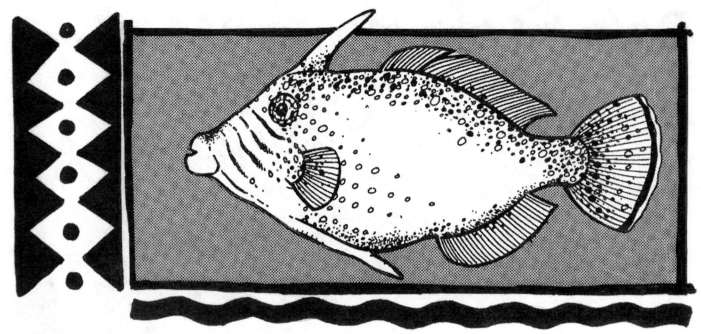

File Fish mysteries.

File fish (´Ōili-´uwī-´uwī) are small multicolored yellow and brown fish with red tails. Every 7-10 years, these fish undergo a tremendous population explosion. At these times the waters are thick with clouds of live file fish. The beaches become littered with file fish remains and huge file fish schools can be found far out at sea. The baby file fish eat so much food in the water that other reef fish starve to death! The ancient Hawaiians believed that whenever this event happened, it foretold the death of a great chief. According to legend a file fish population explosion occurred before the death of Kamehameha I in 1819.

Fish over population at Hanauma Bay

There are more fish concentrated in Hanauma Bay than at any other place on O'ahu because no fishing is allowed here. Most other places around the neighbor Islands also have far fewer fish. Hawaiian reefs support only about 15 percent as many fish as compared to 100 years ago.

The state fish

The fish name *humuhumunukunukuāpua'a* means the fish with "a nose like the snout of a pig". The fish was given this name because of the peculiar noise it makes with its airbladder. Ancient Hawaiians said the sound reminded them of a grunting pig.

The fish was immortalized in "My Little Grass Shack", a famous song written about Hawaii in 1933. Naming it the state fish was the overwhelming choice of the tourist industry. However, many Hawaiian fishermen objected to the choice because they believe the *humuhumu* had very low status among ancient Hawaiians and was not a fit representative.

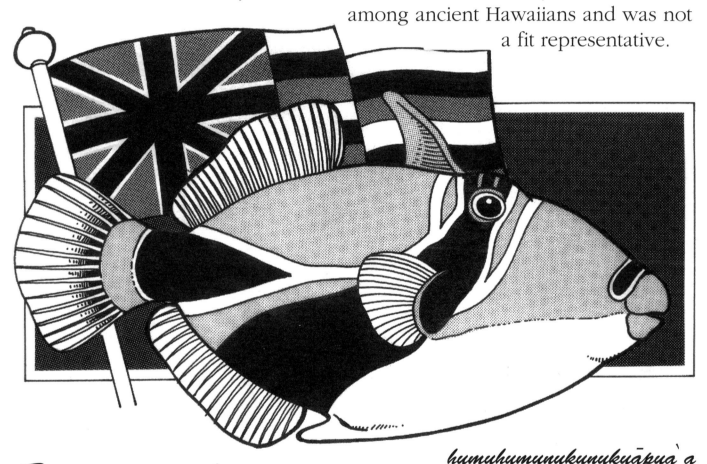

humuhumunukunukuāpua'a

Finger on the trigger

Trigger fish (*humuhumu*) defend themselves by swimming into a hole and raising the strong spine in their front dorsal fin. This spine acts like a anchor sticking into the rock, making it just about impossible to dislodge the fish. This big spine is propped in place by a small bone or "trigger" that holds it in place. In order to lower its spine, the fish must release its "trigger" first.

Gun-Sight-Eyes.

The long stiff body of the trumpet fish (*nuhu*) is not very maneuverable, so it lies motionless in the water hovering above the reef trying to act inconspicuous. The trumpet fish slowly lines up its gun-sight eyes and long snout with some unsuspecting prey. Trumpet fish don't actually bite their prey. They suck them in like a powerful vacuum cleaner. To survive they must nab their prey on the first strike.

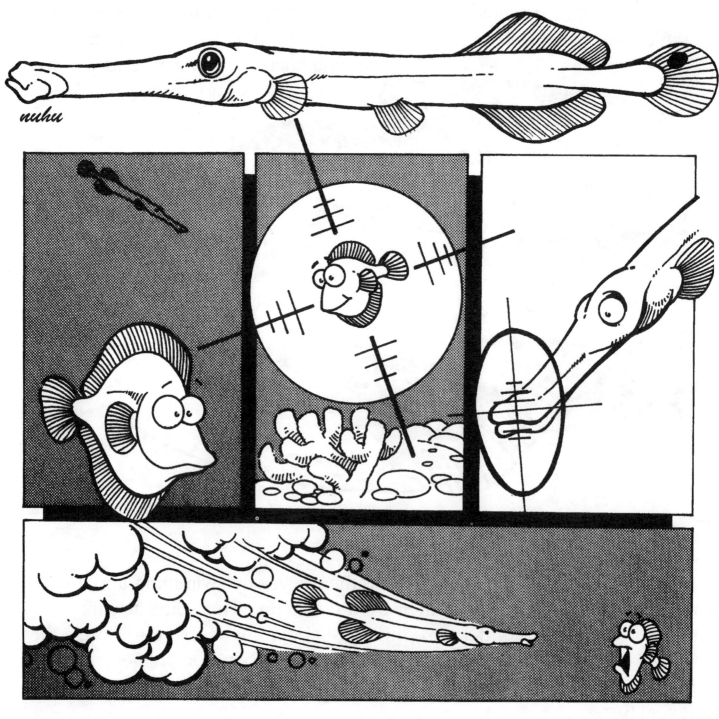

nuhu

Trumpet Fish have strange snouts